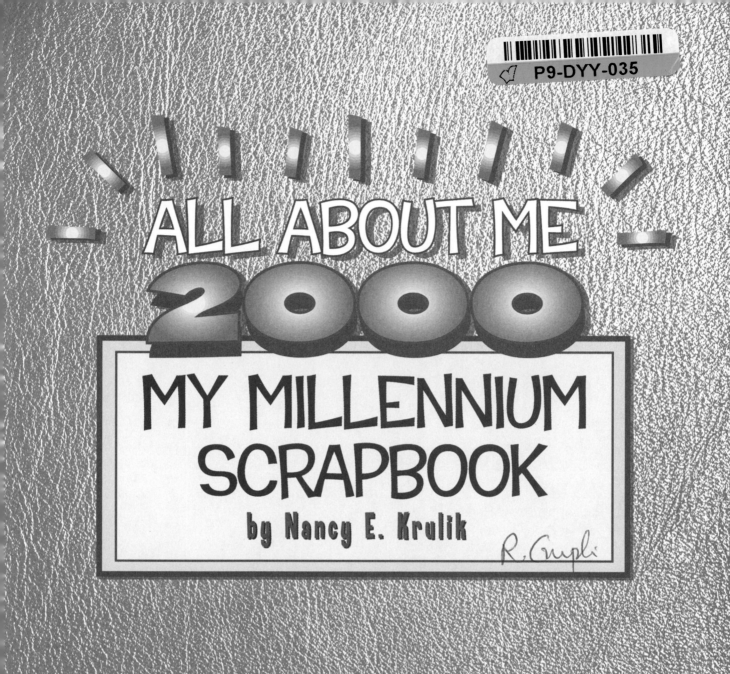

ALL ABOUT ME
2000

MY MILLENNIUM SCRAPBOOK

by Nancy E. Krulik

Scholastic Inc.
New York   Toronto   London   Auckland   Sydney
Mexico City   New Delhi   Hong Kong

Art Direction/Design by Karen Hudson
Spot Illustrations by Cathy Nolan

ISBN 0-439-14608-9

12 11 10 9 8 7 6 5 4 3 2   9/9 0 1 2 3 4/0

Printed in the U.S.A.

First Scholastic printing, December 1999

24

Happy New Year! 2000

Happy New Year! Welcome to the year 2000! It's not just the beginning of a new year, it's the start of a whole new millennium! How cool is that?

Here's what I did to ring in the new millennium.

_____.
_____.
_____.
_____.
_____.

Place pictures of yourself celebrating New Year's Eve here.

This is what I looked like at the start of the new millennium.

Place your
photo here.

These are my vital statistics on January 1, 2000:

I am_____feet_____inches tall.

I weigh_____pounds.

I wear size_____.

I am missing_____teeth.

My shoes are size_____.

My address is

_____

_____

_____.

My phone number is

_____.

MY MILLENNIUM FAMILY TREE

Place pictures of your family here.

GRANDMOTHER

GRANDFATHER

GRANDMOTHER

GRANDFATHER

PARENT

PARENT

SIBLING

ME

SIBLING

FOUR-LEGGED FRIENDS

I have_____pets.

These are the kinds of animals I have:

_____.

Their names are

_____.

Here is a picture I drew of my pets.

My favorite thing to do with my pets is

_____ .

I really love it when my pets

_____ .

Place photos of
your pets here.

Around Town

My neighborhood is the best there is. My favorite part of my neighborhood is our _____.

The best place to play is
_____.

I like to ride my bike to
_____.

When my family goes out to dinner, I always ask to eat at
_____.

When we go there, I always order
_____.

Sometimes, my parents drag me to _____.

I would much rather _____.

On rainy days, I love to
_____.

But when the sun is shining, you can usually find me
_____.

Draw a map of your neighborhood here.

CURRENT EVENTS 2000

The mayor of my town/city is_____.

The governor of my state is_____.

The president of the United States is

_____.

The vice president of the United States is

_____.

Here's what's new in the news:

_____.
_____.
_____.
_____.
_____.
_____.
_____.
_____.
_____.
_____.
_____.
_____.
_____.
_____.

Place headlines from
the newspaper here.

SCHOOL 2000!

The name of my school is _____.

I am in _____ grade.

My classroom number is _____.

There are _____ kids in my class. _____ are girls and _____ are boys.

My teachers' names are _____ and _____.

What I really like about them is

_____.

My favorite subjects are

_____

_____,

but I really don't like _____ all that much.

We went on lots of field trips this year. These are some of the places we visited:

_____

_____

_____.

The best assembly this year was

_____.

The best meal they served in the cafeteria was the

_____.

The worst meal they served in the cafeteria was the

_____.

These are the kids in my class.
Place your class picture and other pictures of your
classmates and teachers here.

Friends
... That's What It's All About!

My best friend is _____.

My funniest friend is _____.

My most shy friend is _____.

My loudest friend is _____.

My most talented friend is _____.

My best-dressed friend is _____.

My smartest friend is _____.

My most athletic friend is _____.

My coolest friend is _____.

This is my best friend.

Place your best friend's
photo here.

Here are my friends and me being silly.

Place photo here.

Meet the future stars of the new millennium.

Place photo here.

The gang's all here!

Place photo here.

Place photo here.

Place photo here.

Place photo here.

These are the jokes and riddles that are going around in the year 2000.

The best joke: _____
_____
_____
_____

The worst joke: _____
_____
_____
_____

The most repeated joke:_____
_____
_____
_____

The joke nobody gets:_____
_____
_____
_____

The joke I wish I had told first: _____
_____
_____
_____

Here's a joke I made up:_____
_____
_____
_____

2000
A Year in Movies

My favorite movie of the year 2000 was
_____.

I liked it because_____
_____
_____
_____.

The funniest movie I saw this year was
_____
_____.

The scariest movie I saw this year was
_____.

The movie I saw the most times in 2000 was
_____.

When I go to the movies, I like to munch on
_____.

My favorite actor is_____.
What I like about him is _____
_____.

My favorite actress is _____.
What I like about her is_____
_____.

My all-time favorite movie character is
_____.

If I could meet any movie star it would be
_____.

Place your movie stubs and
pictures of your favorite stars here.

What's on

Here are the TV shows I watch during the week.

Monday _____

_____

Tuesday _____

_____

Wednesday _____

_____

Thursday _____

_____

Friday _____

_____

Saturday _____

_____

Sunday _____

_____

My all-time favorite TV show is

_____.

My favorite cartoon show is

_____.

My favorite new show for the year 2000 is

_____.

the Tube

My favorite commercial is

_____.

I don't like the commercial for

_____.

My favorite TV stars are

_____.

If I could be on any show, it would be

_____

_____.

Place pictures of your favorite TV stars here.

Rockin' and Rollin'

My favorite CD of the year 2000 is _____
_____.

What I like about it is
_____.

My favorite group is _____
_____.

My favorite singer is _____
_____.

My favorite song is _____
_____.

I love to sing along with this song: _____
_____.

This is the radio station I listen to: _____.

If I could start my own band, I would call it
_____.

This is who would be in my band with me:
_____
_____
_____
_____
_____
_____
_____.

Copy the lyrics to your favorite song here.

_____

_____

_____

_____

_____

_____

_____

_____

_____

_____

Place pictures of your
favorite bands and singers here.

Drop Everything and Read!

My favorite author is _____.

He/she writes books about _____.

The best book I read all year was _____.

I liked it because _____.

The best part was when _____

_____.

I really like this series of books: _____

_____

The books in the series are about _____

_____.

Here's where I like to do my reading:

_____

If I could write a book, I would call it

_____

It would be about_____

_____

_____

_____

_____

_____

_____

_____

_____.

Here are some drawings I made of the things that happened in my favorite book.

Draw your pictures here.

COOL CLOTHES

These are the things no closet should be without in the year 2000.

_____
_____
_____
_____
_____
_____
_____
_____
_____
_____

Place pictures of your favorite fashionable clothing here.

2000: WHAT'S HOT

Here's what everyone is doing and saying.

_____
_____
_____
_____
_____
_____
_____
_____
_____
_____
_____
_____
_____
_____
_____
_____
_____
_____
_____
_____
_____
_____
_____

WHAT'S NOT

These fads are so last millennium!

_____
_____
_____
_____
_____
_____
_____
_____
_____
_____
_____
_____
_____
_____
_____
_____
_____
_____
_____
_____
_____
_____
_____

This year, the hot new toy is the _____.
Place picture of toy here.

The best toy I received all year is my

_____.

The toy I wish I had gotten is the

_____.

My favorite toy of all time is my

_____.

Place picture of your favorite toy here.

When my friends and I all get together, we like to play with our

_____.

2000 was the year that I finally gave away my

_____.

I am really getting great at a video/computer game called

_____.

My high score so far is

_____.

This is a toy I designed for the new millennium.
Draw a picture here.

COLLECTING
IN THE MILLENNIUM!

This year, everyone seems to be collecting
_____.

I collect _____.

I have _____ of them in my collection.

My favorite one is the _____.

The thing in my collection that is worth the most is my
_____.

This is what I would love to add to my collection:
_____.

In the new millennium, I would like to start collecting
_____

and _____.

Here is a photograph of me with my collection.

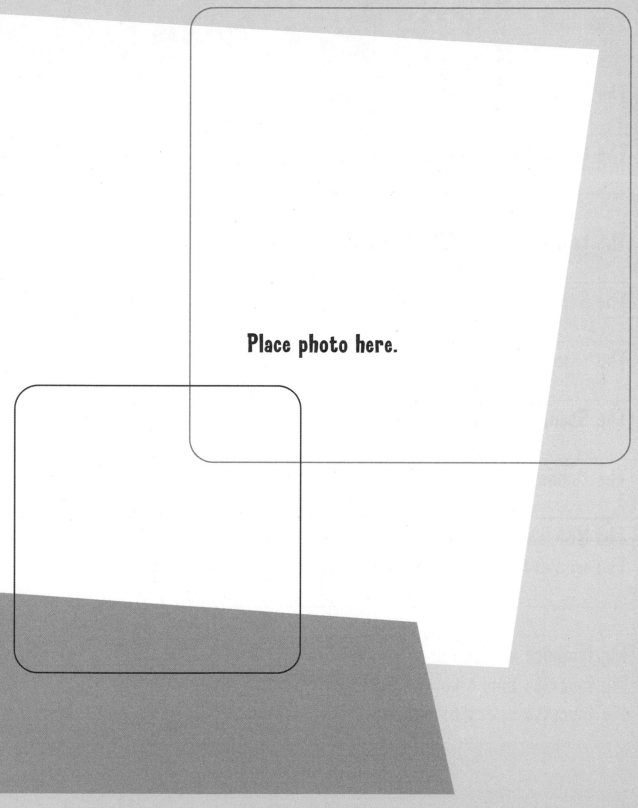

Place photo here.

SPORTS 2000

The teams in the 2000 World Series were the
_____ and the _____.
The World Series champs were the
_____.

The teams in the 2000 Super Bowl were the
_____ and the _____.
The Super Bowl champs were the _____
_____.

The teams in the 2000 Stanley Cup series were the
_____ and the _____.
The Stanley Cup champs were the _____
_____.

The teams in the NBA championship series were the
_____ and the _____.
The NBA champs were the _____.
The winners of the World Cup soccer games were from
_____.

My favorite athlete is _____.
My favorite sport to watch is _____.
My favorite sport to play is _____.

Place team logos and
pictures of your favorite players here.

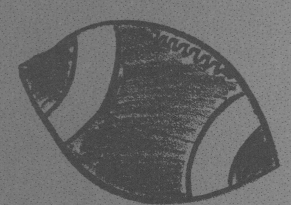

VACATIONS

I've been on the move in 2000!

I went on vacation to _____ .

The people who traveled with me are _____

_____ .

We left our house on _____ , 2000.

We traveled by _____

_____ .

We stayed at _____ .

The coolest thing I saw while on vacation was the _____

_____ .

I wish we'd had more time to look at the _____

_____ .

The souvenirs I brought home with me are _____

_____

_____ .

Place souvenirs from your trip (postcards, napkins with restaurant names on them, business cards, and more) here.

Place photos from your vacation here.

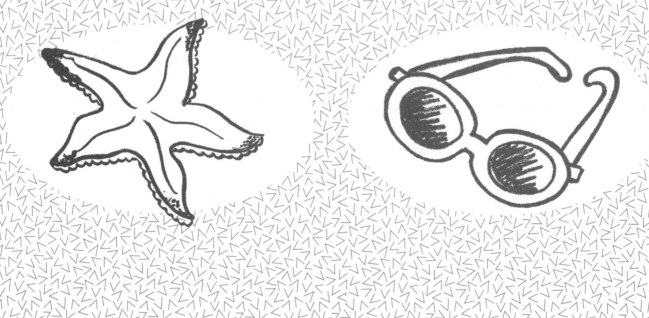

Happy Birthday to Me!

In 2000 I turned _____ years old.

I had my birthday party at _____

_____.

I celebrated my big day with these friends:

_____

_____

_____

_____

_____

These were some of my birthday presents:

_____

_____

_____

_____

This is what my birthday cake looked like.
Draw a picture of your cake here.

Place photos from your
birthday party here.

GONE CAMPING!

My camp is named _____.

Our camp colors are _____.

My counselors' names are _____

_____.

These are the kids in my group:_____

_____

_____

_____

My favorite activity is _____

_____.

This is my swimming group: _____

_____

_____

_____ tells the best ghost stories.

This summer was the first time that I ever

_____.

40

Place small arts-and-crafts projects,
photos, and other camp things here.

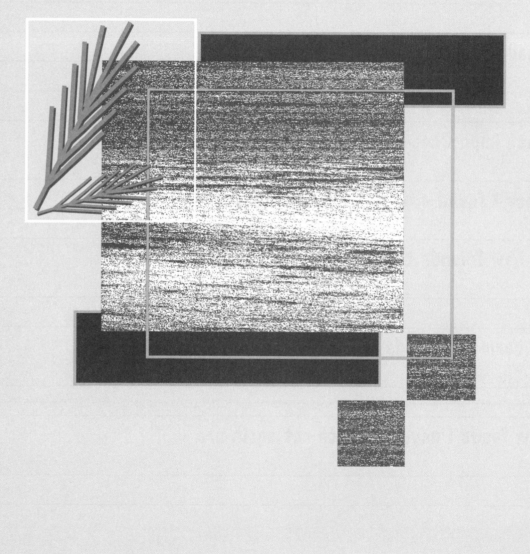

I'M SO PROUD OF ME!

The year 2000 was the first year that I was able to

_____

_____ .

That made me really proud because _____

_____

_____ .

The most important thing I learned in 2000 was

_____ .

This year I found a new hobby. It is _____

_____ .

I made new friends this year. They are

_____

_____ .

I tried some new foods in 2000. The new foods I love are

_____

_____ .

The new foods I never want to eat again are

_____

_____ .

Looking in the CRYSTAL BALL

I can't wait until I am _____ years old.

That's when I'll be able to_____

_____

_____.

When I grow up, I want to be a _____.

When I am a parent, I will always let my kids _____

_____.

I will never ask my kids to _____

_____.

This is what I think I will look like when I am a grown-up.
Draw your picture here.

The Future's Up to Me

These are my hopes for the new millennium.

_____
_____
_____
_____
_____
_____
_____
_____
_____
_____
_____
_____
_____
_____
_____
_____
_____
_____
_____
_____
_____
_____

GOALS

DREAMS

SCHOOL

WHAT'S NEXT?

These are my resolutions for the year 2001:

_____

_____

_____

_____

_____

_____

_____

_____

_____

_____

_____

_____

_____

_____

_____

_____

_____

_____

_____

_____

_____

_____

_____

Place additional photos here.

Place additional photos here.

Place additional photos here.